The [...]

THE HAND-OFF

A Mother-in-law/Daughter-in-law Relationship Guide

By Elizabeth Winn

1

The Hand-Off

The Hand-Off

Acknowledgments

- I want to thank my husband Sean for always cheering me on. For the better part of my life, you have been by my side and my greatest support and fan. Thank you hon. I love you.
- A big thanks to my son, Taylor, who poured his creative gift into the cover of this book. It's perfectly beautiful. Thank you son. And to my daughter Elin, for your honesty, sensitivity, humor and friendship. You mean the absolute world to me.
- To Madeline, my Ruth. Thank you for loving Taylor as you do. Handing him off to you was easy and a privilege.
- To Saundra, my mother-in-law. Thank you for loving me as your own for all these years. You did a brilliant job at handing Sean off to me. I couldn't have asked for a better MIL. I love you very much.
- To the person who has had my back since 7th grade. Trac, your friendship nourishes my soul like no other. What a place this world would be if everyone had a friend like you. I am blessed.
- Thank you to Deb Bostwick who gave her gift of editing to this project. Deb, you know my voice and did a wonderful job in keeping it strong and clear while perfecting the writing. Thank you for your friendship and all you gave to make The Hand-Off a success. I hope to work with you again soon.
- And to the nurse at Children's Mercy Hospital. Thank you for seeing something unique in my relationship with Madeline that prompted your encouragement to write this book. I hope I can find you and get it into your hands.

The Hand-Off

Chapters

The Hand-Off

Chapter One

Laying the Groundwork

It was a very exciting day for me as I sat in the waiting room anticipating the arrival of my very first grandbaby. Penny Evelyn was being delivered four weeks early due to a condition called gastroschisis, which finds the intestines developing outside the abdomen. Because of this, Penny had been closely monitored for over a month with tri-weekly appointments involving high-tech sonograms and heart monitoring.

The Hand-Off

Due to recently starting a new job, our son Taylor was unable to accompany our daughter-in-law, Madeline, to these appointments so I began to make the three times a week trip to Children's Mercy Hospital with her. I found it fascinating to watch Penny grow and really enjoyed the time I was getting to spend with Madeline. Because of so many visits, we came to know the staff of nurses, doctors, and sonographers very well.

As I sat in the waiting room that day, the nurse who had been assigned to Madeline for the appointments leading up to Penny's birth came through the double doors and saw me sitting there. She was leaving for the day and invited me to walk with her to the elevators. As she and I began to walk, she said *"Elizabeth...the girls in the back and I have been talking and we all agree you should write a book on how to have a relationship with your daughter-in-law. We have watched how much you and*

The Hand-Off

Madeline love each other and we want to know how to have that same kind of relationship when our sons get married. I have a 14-year-old son, and I am so afraid that when he gets married I will lose him. You know that saying 'A son is a son till he takes a wife and a daughter is a daughter for all of her life'....this really makes me feel sad because I think it is so true!"

Her comment took me totally off guard and I began to laugh it off, but realized she was very serious. We went on to talk a few moments about the mother-in-law/daughter-in-law subject and I thanked her for her kind words about Madeline and me before saying good-bye. As a result of that conversation came the writing of this book.

The Hand-Off

I have often thought about what exactly stood out in my relationship with Madeline to the women working at the hospital. We certainly did not go in with an agenda of "Now, how can we show how much we love one another today?" When I boil it down, I think what they observed was genuine love and respect for one another.

My Ruth

There is a story in the Bible about a mother-in-law named Naomi and her daughter-in-law, Ruth.

The relationship between Naomi and Ruth was special. Ruth loved her mother-in-law so much she chose to follow Naomi as she returned to her homeland after her husband and both sons, one being Ruth's husband, died. Instead of staying in her own homeland, with her own family, Ruth chose to go with Naomi. You may or may not be familiar with Ruth's response to Naomi's insistence she stay with her family, but I have always felt it gave a beautiful picture of Ruth's heart.

Ruth 1:16-17

16 But Ruth replied, "Don't urge me to leave you or to turn back from you. Where you go I will go, and where you stay I will stay. Your people will be my people and your God my God. 17 Where you die I will die, and there I will be buried. May the LORD deal with me, be it ever so severely, if even death separates you and me."

> If any relationship is going to be a good one, there is going to be intention from both parties involved.

The Hand-Off

As a woman whose faith is everything to me, I had spent a lot of time asking God to bless our son, Taylor, with a wonderful wife. I loved the heart of Ruth so I began to ask God for a Naomi/Ruth relationship with whomever He brought into Taylor's life. Enter Madeline Leigh Cook.

Taylor and Madeline met in an internship in our hometown. She was originally from Keller, Texas and we soon found out Madeline spent a lot of her childhood with her grandparents who lived blocks from our home in Garland, Texas, when Taylor was little. We laughed at the possibility of them playing at the same park during their childhood. Our whole family fell in love with Madeline, including our daughter, Elin, who always had a strong opinion on who her older brother dated. It did not take long for us to see that Taylor and Madeline were meant for one another and soon they were engaged to be married.

The Hand-Off

Sometime after the kids got engaged, I wrote Madeline a note in her birthday card and mentioned I had prayed for a Naomi/Ruth relationship with Taylor's wife and that I felt God had answered my prayer. I was so happy when Madeline shared with me after reading my note that she too had asked God for a Naomi/Ruth relationship with her future mother-in-law. I feel like she and I have both guarded our relationship and been protective of it because we both believe it was meant to be. We have a good, healthy relationship, but not just because we are two amazing women! We have a good, healthy relationship because we are intentional about loving the other well. If any relationship is going to be a good one, there is going to be intention from both parties involved. Good relationships just don't happen.

To finish the story of Naomi and Ruth, it shows that not only the love between them, but also the trust Ruth had in Naomi and Naomi's love for

The Hand-Off

Ruth created a powerful example of God's story for each one of us. Because these two women chose to love and work together well, God was able to work His perfect will for the generations upon generations that followed. Now, that's a powerful love!

As I have spoken to several women about this relational subject, I have heard some very heartbreaking stories from both mothers-in-law and daughters-in-law who long for a relationship with each other, but are not sure how to navigate through the pain of the past and move forward. If this is you, this book was written for you. Perhaps you are about to become a mother-in-law or daughter-in-law and you want a healthy relationship with your son's wife or your husband's mother. This book was written for you too.

The Hand-Off

Maybe you are a son, about to become a husband. It is important for you to understand how the health of this relationship, between your mother and your wife, is going to tremendously impact your marriage. It has the power to make it more wonderful or totally miserable. This book was written for you as well, to assist you in understanding the hearts of these two important women in your life and the role you play in helping their relationship be the best it can be.

The title of this book, *The Hand Off*, is a good description of both party's responsibility in making this relationship a success from the very beginning. As a mother, you are passing the baton of your son's heart to his wife. In doing this, you have to completely let go of it. Imagine if you tried to hang on while your son's wife grabbed hold….instead of sprinting on ahead, she would struggle with moving forward as she is forced to drag you along behind her! Ladies…this is not a pretty picture.

The Hand-Off

Moms…we must let go of the baton completely and affirm who we are passing it on to. Wives…we must receive the baton with gratefulness to who we are receiving it from.

I know for some of you there is a lot of pain connected to this relationship. You wish so much it could be better, but you are stuck and not sure how to move forward. My heart truly hurts for you whether you are a mother-in-law or a daughter-in-law. You may have picked up this book to see if you can give it to your mother-in-law or daughter-in-law so they will read it and change! But this book is not about changing the other person. It is all about changing you and at the same time helping you understand her better. I am *for* both of you. My heart's desire is to create empathy in the hearts of both of you. If you can see each other clearly, it can be the beginning of starting again. And if you are just starting out, perhaps this book will help you execute the perfect hand-off!

The Hand-Off

So let's take a closer look at the amazing potential of this important, powerful relationship and the role we play, either as a mother-in-law or daughter-in-law, in making the "hand-off" a successful one!

The Hand-Off

Chapter 1: Reflection

When it comes to your relationship with your current or future mother-in-law or daughter-in-law, how do you view it, what are your thoughts about it, what are your hopes for how it?

What are some things you would like to see change in your relationship with your mother-in-law or daughter-in-law?

Chapter Two

It Takes Two to Tango

Two women. Both love the same man. One has loved him since before he was born. One has allowed love for him to claim her heart. One has been the number one woman in his life since he entered this world. One is invited to move into that spot for the rest of his life. One is asked to let go and move aside. One is asked to consider the love it takes to trust her with him.

Both of these women have a tremendous responsibility to this powerful, at times challenging, wonderful, at moments maddening, beautiful

19

mother-in-law/daughter-in-law relationship. And anything worth having is worth giving our attention and intention to. I think so many of us have entered into this relationship without giving it much thought or attention. We have not considered how this "other woman" might affect our life or how we might affect her life.

As a young woman getting ready to marry my husband, Sean, I just wanted his mom, Saundra, to like me. That was really my only thought. I do not remember giving much thought to what it might be like for her, what she might be feeling as I took her son as my husband. Saundra did a wonderful job of handing off Sean to me, but looking back I wish I had considered her feelings more and been able to express to her how grateful I was for how she prepared him for me.

The Hand-Off

The Gifts Each One Brings

I wonder what would happen to the mother-in-law/daughter-in-law relationship if each would consider how important the other one was to her life. This friendship is one born out of love, the love of a mother for her son and the love of a woman for her man. Each woman is receiving a beautifully wrapped gift in the life of one another.

Wives, you are gaining another mother! You may have a wonderful relationship with your own mother, but what is better

All of a sudden you have someone else to love you

than one mom?...Two! All of a sudden you have someone else to love you, care for you, be there for you, hug you and let you cry, give you tips on cooking, taking care of babies, how to navigate marriage, how to get soap scum off the shower wall, how to make a Barbie cake, how to cook fried okra, and a million other insights that come with living 40 plus years.

Moms, you are gaining a daughter! Now, if you are a mom of only sons....this is even GREATER NEWS! Daughters are awesome! My daughter, Elin, is so amazing and adding Madeline to the mix just made it better! Daughters make wonderful friends who shop with you, get pedicures with you, honestly tell you if you can pull off that cute "young" looking outfit, laugh with you, sit at a coffee shop with you, go antiquing and garage sale shopping. They make great hiking or work out buddies or a host of other stuff that will keep you young at heart!

The Hand-Off

One of the greatest things a daughter-in-law does is keep you updated on your son's life. Taylor never calls me just to chat. My daughter, Elin, calls and texts all the time, just to talk! The reality is, your son is most likely not the best at keeping you updated on what's going on in his life. That is what a daughter-in-law is for! I love this part of my relationship with Madeline because I feel like I know what is going on in Taylor's life. She does not over share or tell me things I have no business knowing,

> **The reality is, your son is most likely not the best at keeping you updated on what's going on in his life.**

but just day to day, life stuff. I feel connected to Taylor through having a relationship with Madeline.

The Hand-Off

So you can see how wonderful this mother-in-law/daughter-in-law connection can be, if both parties can appreciate all the incredible, invaluable, blessings each brings into the relationship. It is truly a beautiful partnership if given the attention and intention it deserves.

A Different Kind of Love

There is a very special love waiting for every mother-in-law and daughter-in-law within this relationship. If each of you intentionally looks for and finds it, this love will become a treasure to you both. The key is realizing, whether you are the mother-in-law or the daughter-in-law, you have the responsibility to learn how the other one needs love from you. In other words, how does love speak to her? In what ways will she receive love best from you?

The Hand-Off

If you are a daughter-in-law, wanting your mother-in-law to feel loved by you, here are a few ideas of how you could go about loving her well.

- Call her, just to chat, about what is happening in your life. This is especially important if you and your husband live a distance away.
- Call her and ask a question about your husband. Something you haven't figured out yet about him, but his mom is sure to know!
- Engage your Mother-in-law in conversation about her life. In doing this you show an interest in who she is as a human being, what she does day to day, what her likes/dislikes are, what books she likes, movies she enjoys, etc. It says, "I value you as a person and want to know about you!"
- Give her a thoughtful gift….especially when there is no occasion!

The Hand-Off

- Ask what might work well for her regarding holiday plans, instead of informing her of what you and your husband will be doing.
- Say the words, "I love you," These are a mother's three favorite words. Don't be afraid of speaking them out loud, writing them in a note, or typing them in a text.

If you are a mother-in-law, wanting your daughter-in-law to feel loved by you, here are a few ideas of how you could go about loving her well.

- Call to check in and see how she is doing. Focus on her, not your son.
- Get to know her taste in clothes, décor, food, favorite restaurants, so that you can buy great gift cards for her!
- Bring her chicken noodle soup when she is sick. And maybe brownies.

The Hand-Off

- Give sincere compliments on her decorating, her cooking, and her mothering. Often!
- Ask what would work best for her and your son regarding holiday plans, letting her know you want to be flexible, knowing they have two families to work with.
- Use affectionate names when talking to her. Sweetheart, Sweet girl, Love, Hon, are a few of my favorites. It speaks of your affection for her, It says "You are more than just a girl in my life…you are my daughter and I love you."

I offer these as just a few ideas, but might I suggest you ask your mother-in-law or your daughter-in-law, a couple of questions. First, "Do you feel loved by me?" and depending on the answer you receive, the second is "What can I do or stop doing to make you feel more loved by me?" This line of questioning might seem cheesy to you, or scare the heebie-jeebies out of you, or require a truckload of humility from you…but I have found when I don't know something about Madeline, the best way to find out is to ask her.

This authenticity in relationship is missing in a lot of mother-in-law/daughter-in-law relationships. Being willing to be vulnerable and authentic can help break down walls and allow conversation, that you thought would be difficult, to begin to flow more easily. The result of a vulnerable, honest, loving conversation, where both of you are being quick to listen and slow to speak, can be a turning point in a troubled relationship.

This is NOT a Competition

The powerful love of a mother and the passionate love of a wife are two very different parts of love. A man has the privilege of experiencing both sides of love within the walls of both these relationships. If done well, a mother has the power to love her son in a

> It's imperative that both mother and wife understand…this is NOT a competition.

power to love her son in a way that prepares him for the love of his wife. A mother releases him to fully give his whole self, his whole heart, to loving his wife. If not done well, a mother has the power to imprison her son, keeping him from being able to love his wife fully, feeling like he has to split his affection between two women. It's imperative that both mother and wife understand…this is NOT a competition.

The Hand-Off

Mothers…the unwavering love your son feels for you is one of gratefulness, loyalty, and protection. You are the first woman he bonds with in life. You are a place of safety and warmth. You are fierce when it comes to protecting him. Your heart is full of nurturing, maternal instincts that have had a profound effect on his life.

The health of this love is displayed in your understanding that you are going to be called to completely let go of him when his wife comes along. You live with this understanding as you are raising him. This doesn't mean loss of relationship, love, loyalty, affection, appreciation, or gratefulness with him. It means he moves forward in the strength, wisdom, and health of the love you have poured into him, and pours it out into his wife. He is confident in loving her well, because you have loved him well.

The Hand-Off

In other words, he doesn't worry about you. He knows you are secure in his love for you. Your identity is not wrapped up in being his mom. Motherhood is a part of who you are, not your entire identity. This is how you let him go in the way his wife needs you to. When you let him go in this way, you don't lose your son…you gain a daughter.

Wives…if your man loves his mother well, he will love you well. Watch the way in which he speaks to her and listen to the way in which he speaks of her, in conversation. The attitude your man has towards his mother will greatly impact his relationship with you. You are not in competition with her. She is your greatest ally. When your heart can honor her for what she has poured into your husband to help make him the man he is, it can rest in knowing there is no need to vie for his affection or love because you already have it fully. Her influence on his life has a lot to do with why you love him. Loving her, for loving him the way in which she did his whole life, is not only a gift to her, but to your man as well.

One Important Question

Have you ever given much thought to what it is like for others to live on the other side of you? What is it like to wake up to you, to be married to you, to come home to you? What is it like to be your son, to be your daughter? What is it like to be your mother, to be your father, to be your friend? What is it like to be in an argument with you? What is it like to sit in a work meeting with you? What is it like to be your boss? What is it like…to be your mother-in-law? What is it like… to be your daughter-in-law?

The Hand-Off

If you are like me, my first response when I was encouraged to ask this question to people in my life was, "Ugh. I'm not sure I want to know." But in reality, what an amazing question this is, especially in the context of the mother-in-law/daughter-in-law relationship:

"WHAT IS IT LIKE TO LIVE ON THE OTHER SIDE OF ME?"

Sit with that one for just a moment. Take some time to consider. Don't rush past the depth of this question.

Mothers-in-law…what is it like for your daughter-in-law to live on the other side of you? What does the expression on your face speak to her when she walks into your home? How does your tone of voice frame your words? What is it like for her to live on the other side of your questions?

The Hand-Off

Daughters-in-law…what is it like for your mother-in-law to live on the other side of you? Does she look forward to visits to your home? Is conversation with you effortless, or does she have to walk on eggshells so she doesn't offend? Does she feel resistance from you, or does she know you welcome her presence?

It is a powerful question. Do you have the nerve to ask this question to one another? The important thing about asking this question is the heart behind it. The rules are - you can't say anything in response to their answer. No defending your self. No explaining why you act the way you do. No coming back with, "Well, if you did such n such, I wouldn't be like that." Nope. No talking. Just listening. Listening only. Talking zero. Get it?

The Hand-Off

The temptation is to be willing to ask the question, if and only if, you get to answer the question from them too. But for the question to do any good in your life, to bring about any change in you, to make the relationship better between you and her, you have to ask it without wanting the opportunity to answer it. Make sense?

If you will ask it, let her answer it, and walk away, committed to considering all she said, it will change you. It will change your relationship. She will expect

---

"WHAT IS IT LIKE TO LIVE ON THE OTHER SIDE OF ME?"

---

you to say "So, now…would you like to ask me the same question? Hmmmm??" But when you don't, and all you say is, "Thank you, I

35

The Hand-Off

really appreciate your honesty", you will have made inroads you never
knew were possible.

I dare you.

Ask it.

Chapter 2: Reflection

Being brutally honest with yourself, how do you think your mother-in-law or daughter-in-law would answer the question, "What is it like to live on the other side of me?" She would say I am....?

If you have been courageous enough to ask her the question, what changes are you needing to make in order to make it easier for her to live on the other side of you?

The Hand-Off

Chapter 3

My Baby is Getting Married!

I can remember the day I became a mother like it was yesterday. I was twenty-two years old and my dream of becoming a mom was coming true. Sean and I had gotten married nine months ago, and here we were about to become parents. Honeymoon baby. Ya gotta love it.

Taylor Sean Winn entered this world at 3:20 pm on a Sunday afternoon. My heart was never to be the same. Every mother knows what I mean. Your heart stops beating for yourself and in one breathtaking moment, it begins to beat for someone else. All of a sudden you would give your life

The Hand-Off

for this tiny person. Your needs seemingly become less important as this little human fills every corner of your being. It's a wonderful, beautiful, fierce kind of connection.

We had no idea what gender our baby would be before he was born. We really didn't care, as long as he was healthy. When my doctor announced "It's a boy!" I was so happy. A son. A little boy. I couldn't wait!

Taylor was a really good little guy. He was all boy and had a precious little caring heart. He loved his friends and loved activity and kept me on my toes. He and I spent every day together, running our errands, staying at the house, playing outside. He was my little buddy and I absolutely loved being his mom.

The Hand-Off

Taylor and I had similar personalities so we got along pretty well as he grew up. Conversation came easily for us and I would say we had a good relationship all throughout his growing up years.

I seemed to always be keenly aware I was raising someone's husband. I would tell Taylor, "Your wife is not going to want to pick your clothes up off the floor, so pick them up!" I would wait for him to open the door for me if we were out together. I held a tight reign on him if he was upset, letting him know he could not fly off the handle just because he was angry. I would warn him in conversation. "Buddy, you are about to cross the line in the way you are speaking to me, better get ahold of yourself." He knew there was a right way to speak to a woman and yelling at her was not acceptable. I tried to raise him with her in mind, knowing I would hand him off one day.

The Hand-Off

I remember his first date. He asked a classmate to be his date for Homecoming his freshman year of high school. Emily was her name. I can remember pressing his dress shirt, making sure his dress pants were long enough and not high waters, picking out one of Sean's ties for him to wear. He looked sharp. We dropped him off with a corsage, a mouth full of braces and an acne spotted face, armed with instructions of how to act on a date. It was a success. One down, many more to follow.

At some point in college, Taylor decided to stop dating until he was ready to settle down and get married. It was one of the best decisions he made at that time in his life. He was free to have a great co-ed group of friends and enjoy his college years without the pressure of dating. After graduation, he entered an internship for a year and along came Madeline Cook.

The Hand-Off

She's NOT Who I had in Mind

Sharon, a very wise friend of mine, gave me the best advice one day regarding my kids and their future spouses. Sharon said this, "Elizabeth, try really hard to not have a kind of "someone" in mind for your kid's spouse. Don't get in your head a certain personality, or physical look, or a particular kind of family they should come from. Only God knows who is best for them. Only God."

What marvelous advice. I was sure to be disappointed if I had in my mind a specific kind of girl for Taylor and he brought home someone completely opposite of what I imagined. Who wants to feel disappointment from their future Mother-in-law when they meet her? So, I followed Sharon's advice and refused to imagine the type of girl Taylor might end up with. Sharon was right, God knew Madeline was perfect for Taylor and He brought her into his life at the perfect time.

Let me pause for a moment and address this a little deeper. Mom, perhaps you had an "idea" of what would be best for your son

> ## I wasn't what his mother had in mind for her little boy

and your Daughter-in-law turned out to be nothing like your idea. Could it be possible your disappointment showed when meeting her? If so, can I suggest this may have something to do with the distance you feel from her? I have spoken to wives who have told me this very thing. "I wasn't what his mother had in mind for her little boy." You may have been thinking you hid your disappointment well, but if there is strain between you and her and you're unsure why, this may be the underlying issue.

What can be done? Easy, well maybe not super easy, but humble yourself and apologize to her. Tell her you were wrong to have a certain

The Hand-Off

image in your head about who your son would marry. Tell her how glad you are he chose her. Apologize for showing any disappointment and assure her you are not disappointed in his choice. Ask her to forgive you. Sounds simple, but again, an honest, vulnerable, loving conversation can help heal a wound and put you on a new path together.

You may be asking, "But what if I really am disappointed in who my son chose?" Well, this is going to sound harsh but…you're just going to have to get over it. I say that with all due respect, but there really is no other solution if you desire peace in this relationship. What is done is done. She is now his wife. She is your daughter. Your only worthwhile option now is to love her and love her well.

The Hand-Off

Believe me, I know your situation might be like many I have heard about. The "daughter-in-law from hell" who makes life miserable for everyone, but what I am saying is you are only responsible for you. And you have a lot of power in your kindness and love. Use it. There are very few people who can continue to act horribly to someone who is kind to them over and over. Your willingness to show her love and kindness, in spite of her actions, could be the very thing that turns her heart towards you. Believe me, your son will be forever grateful to you.

If I'm being honest, I'd say the weight of a smooth transition sits more with the mother-in-law than the daughter-in-law. Let's face it, you are older, meaning

The weight of a smooth transition sits more with the mother-in-law than the daughter-in-law.

you have been around the block a few times. You are wiser and understand marriage and the work it takes. You can see the big picture more clearly, and hopefully are more emotionally and relationally mature than this young woman who has stolen your son's heart. This doesn't mean she gets a free pass in this relationship, by no means! I'll have plenty to say to her in the next chapter, but it simply means we have a lot of influence on this relationship heading in the right direction. Hopefully your heart is open to using that influence wisely.

No Longer your Baby

One of my biggest pet peeves is when I hear a woman refer to her grown son as her baby. I know what she means, but it still rubs me the wrong way. I asked a friend of mine recently, who is having some pretty serious issues with her daughter-in-law, if she ever referred to her son as her

The Hand-Off

baby in front of her daughter-in-law. She said "Yes…should I not?"

I told her it had always been a pet peeve of mine and maybe it was something that bothered her daughter-in-law. Her response was very telling of her heart, she said, "Oh my, I need to stop doing that!" She wants relationship so badly with her daughter-in-law and I love the fact she is willing to look within and do whatever it takes to improve their relationship.

Here's the truth. He was your baby. Years and years ago he was in your arms, and then toddling around, and then going to school, and then driving a car, and then going on dates, and then going off to college, and then getting married. He is no longer your baby boy. He is her man. He belongs to her. He still loves you, but his heart is now in her hands and she is responsible for it!

The Hand-Off

Some of you want to toss this book across the room. I get it. It's hard. You have a really close relationship with your son and now you feel disconnected from him. You feel like she stole him away from you. You wish for everything to be like it always has been. But it can't be. Your relationship with him has to shift if your son and his wife are going to have a healthy marriage.

These are a few arguments I have heard from many moms:

- "He was mine before he was hers!"
- "I raised him! I know him better!"
- "He will always be my baby boy!"
- "She just has to understand how close he and I are!"
- "He's my best friend!"
- "I feel like she stole him away from me!"

The Hand-Off

She didn't steal him away, she just fell in love with him. She should be his best friend now. You will now be close to her as well as close to him. She will grow to know him better than you, and this is how it should be. He's not your baby boy anymore, he is her man - just like you raised him to be. A man who knows how to love a woman well because you taught him how. A man who is ready to treat his wife with respect because he has treated you with respect. A man who is equipped to be a good husband because he has had a great mom. You have accomplished what you set out to do! You are awesome! You took a little boy and raised him to be a wonderful man. It's now time to change positions, from the number one spot into the number two spot. And moving with grace and love is the only way to do it.

At Taylor and Madeline's rehearsal dinner, I came up with the idea of having a little bit of fun with this truth of needing to hand Taylor off to

The Hand-Off

Madeline. There was another person in the room that night who was doing a hand-off too and that was Madeline's dad, Casey. He was handing Madeline over to Taylor and letting go completely, as I was handing over Taylor to Madeline and letting go completely as well.

Casey had been the number one man in Madeline's life up until now, and I had been the number one woman in Taylor's life. So in celebration of this "moving to the number two spot", I made Casey and I sashes to wear declaring #2 man and #2 woman. Looking back on it, it sounds really corny, but it also was a public declaration of us both knowing the place we now held in our kids life. Corny, but true.

As you find a home in this new position, it will be much easier on your heart if you view it as not a loss, but a gain. When Taylor married

The Hand-Off

Madeline, she was a gift to our entire family. She belongs to us now. She is family. She is a daughter to Sean and me. She is a sister to Elin. Taylor became a son and brother to Madeline's wonderful family. This is the way it works. And if the hand-off is done well, it's a beautiful blending of two families.

As a mom we have a choice to view it not as a "demotion" but a "promotion"…a "promotion" to becoming a mother-in-law and holding that role very close to our heart. It's a wonderful advancement! We are gaining relationship, not losing it. We are expanding our hearts to welcome another member into our family. And so much of the success of this transition depends on our attitude and heart towards it.

The Hand-Off

Some of you want to love your daughter-in-law well but haven't been given the opportunity because of her wounded heart. She came with a wall built around her heart and no matter how hard you have tried, it's been impossible to break through. Can I just say....please keep trying. Please don't give up. Please keep pouring love into her even if you never receive any back. Believe me when I say, she feels it and it feels good. She may not be able to admit it or know how to open her heart's door to you, but she needs you to keep loving, keep pursuing, keep giving. She won't be able to deny your love forever. Slowly but surely it will begin to seep through. It may take a lifetime, depending on how deeply she is wounded, but your life will be blessed as you learn to love unconditionally this woman your son loves.

Before closing this chapter, let me just give a big thank you to my own mother-in-law, Saundra. I gave very little thought to her role as I married

The Hand-Off

Sean. I liked her, she seemed to like me, and we moved forward in relationship. What I realize now is she moved out of her #1 spot with grace and very little fanfare and it was because of this that she and I have had a lovely relationship for 30 years. She led the way with love. She has never seen me as her daughter-in-law but as her daughter. She always told me she loved me as her own, but I don't think I fully believed it until Taylor married Madeline. She has loved me well and been a wonderful mother to me and I love her with all my heart. I have been richly blessed.

So yes…as the title of this chapter declares "Your baby is getting married!"…and it's a good thing. A blessed event. Even if it happened years ago, even if maybe you had someone else in mind, even if it challenges you to see your son, not as your baby, but as her man now, even if you feel loss…remember always…you have gained a precious gift wrapped in a beautiful package of a daughter-in-law. If you are just

The Hand-Off

starting out or needing to make some adjustments after many years, make sure she knows how much you treasure the gift of her.

Chapter 3: Reflection

Mother-in-laws…what stood out to you in this chapter? Did you see yourself in any of the areas I spoke about?

What do you plan to start doing, or stop doing, to make your relationship with your daughter-in-law better?

The Hand-Off

Have you completely let go of your son's heart and handed it off to your daughter-in-law? If not, what is holding you back from doing it? What is one thing you can do to let completely go?

The Hand-Off

Chapter Four

I'm Going to the Chapel!

No matter if you are on your way to the chapel or took that trip years ago, it's an exciting moment in a woman's life when her dreams of getting married come true. Prince Charming has finally been found and the life you always imagined is right around the corner. It's the day when so many things change. You become a Mrs. and take his name. You make covenant vows until death parts you. You become the "lady" of the house and whether you are aware of it or not, you replace someone as "the #1 woman" in your new husband's life.

The Hand-Off

This chapter is written to help open your eyes and heart to how you can make this "hand-off" a success, or if the hand-off happened years ago, how you can make it better as a daughter-in-law. I said in the last chapter that the weight of making a successful hand-off sits with the Mother-in-law, but that is not to say you don't have a huge responsibility in this relationship as well. Just like there are truths a mother-in-law has to discover, there are truths for you to consider and live by as well.

He was Hers Before He was Yours

Your husband belonged to her long before he belonged to you. If you have children you can empathize with this. If you aren't a mother yet, it may be more difficult to put yourself in her position. Like we talked about in the last chapter, mothers can sometimes struggle with thinking

The Hand-Off

differently about their child as they get older. To a mother, her child will always be her child. It can be challenging to see them as an adult and let them go to make a life for themselves. It's hard for every mother, but more so for some than others.

As a daughter-in-law, understanding the truth that he captured her heart long before he captured yours, is a gift to her and to your man. This understanding brings with it patience, kindness, and a sensitivity to her journey. Her history with him is full of memories that light up her face when she ponders them. She has so many stories to tell of his cuteness, his antics, and triumphs. All of which must be honored and appreciated by you as you take your place beside him.

The Hand-Off

Someone has helped him become the man he is today. His kindness, his ability to treat you well, his lovability and the other attributes that drew you towards him just didn't happen. A wise wife considers the love and sacrifice that went into forming her husband into the man he is. And through that consideration, gratefulness begins to take root inside her heart and gratefulness translates into that patience, kindness, and sensitivity spoken of earlier.

Graciousness Goes a Long Way

One word I think of to describe a woman who understands the truth of "he was hers before he was mine" is graciousness. When I looked up this word for its definition, I found words like merciful, compassionate, delicacy, tact, good taste, courtesy, and generosity of spirit. Do you want to be described as gracious? I certainly do.

The Hand-Off

Graciousness is required from a daughter-in-law for a successful hand-off. Graciousness leads the way into the number one spot in her man's life with a gentle, tactful, merciful,

> **Graciousness: merciful, compassionate, delicacy, tact, good taste, courtesy, and generosity of spirit**

compassionate, generosity of spirit. And when she walks in graciousness, her mother-in-law will adore her. Her mother-in-law would climb a mountain to bring her a lemonade. Her mother-in-law would bend over backwards to help her in anyway she can. She will have won her mother-in-law's heart as she graciously says "Thank you for this man you prepared for me."

The Hand-Off

Be gracious.

Easier Said than Done

For just a moment, let's talk about why this may be difficult for some of you. I am well aware that I am speaking to many wounded hearts and the person who wounded you was your own mother. So your trust in "mothers" isn't at an all time high. And when you hear me talk about treating your mother-in-law with all this kindness, love, and grace, you cringe. You cringe because all you want to do is build a big wall around your heart so that this "other kind of mother" that is now in your life, won't hurt you.

Your self-preservation skills kick in as you are faced with another mother figure, and the only thing you are sure of about mothers is they

The Hand-Off

aren't all June Cleaver or Carol Brady. I can just hear some of you asking, "Who are June Cleaver and Carol Brady?" They are Hollywood's persona of what a good mom is. Their life is all about their kids, they keep immaculate homes, they are always smiling and available, they wear high heels when they vacuum, and they bake cookies (also in heels). They aren't stressed out and impatient, they never yell, they never wound, and they certainly never leave.

If I am speaking to you, let me just say, my heart aches for you. I wish you had a different story. I wish you had felt loved, wanted, and secure in your mother's love. But can I offer you some hope? It's not too late to experience those things. This woman who has loved your man for all his days wants to embrace you. She deserves the opportunity to wrap you up in the love she has poured into him his entire life. She is excited for a relationship with you. Are you willing to take a risk and trust her with your heart? Will it be perfect? No relationship is, but it can be healthy and can be used to heal your wounded heart. Won't you let her in? If you have an awesome man, chances are he has an awesome mom. Chances are, she wants to love you well. Everything can change today.

As I finish up writing this last paragraph I am struck with the thought, what about the daughter-in-law who wants to take the risk...is willing to let her in...but she doesn't seem to want anything to do with you. To you I say...love her well anyway. She may be really struggling to let go. Help her see that you aren't taking her son away. Tell her how much you appreciate all she did to make him the man he is. Do kind things for her. Speak kindly to her and about her. Call her to chat. Ask if you can do

Love and kindness are weapons to use against a hardened or fearful heart

anything for her. Send a card to her for no occasion. Love and kindness are weapons to use against a hardened or fearful heart. They have the power to melt away fear, anger, frustration, miscommunication, hurt feelings, and a truckload of other things keeping your mother-in-law an arm's length away. Try it. It certainly can't hurt.

What a Resource She is!

When Taylor and Madeline first got married, I remember Madeline talking to me about some things going on with Taylor…nothing inappropriate or out of line…she was just trying to figure him out. I would ask her, "Do you need me just to listen, or do you want to know my thoughts?" Most of the time she wanted to know what I thought. Wise girl!- Why? Because at that point in their relationship, she knew I understood Taylor with a lot more depth than she did. And she knew I might be able to bring some perspective and shed some light on why he did the things he did.

If you are just starting out, keep in mind your mother-in-law is a valuable resource to you. She knows your man very well. She has a different frame of reference as his mother and could shed light on some things you are struggling in understanding about him. If you are struggleing with this advice, thinking, "I'm married to the man, I think I know him better than her!" may I suggest this is true in many ways but in some ways she might understand "the why" behind his behavior or perspective. This new knowledge could help draw you closer to him, and therefore be a better wife. There will come a day when she does not know him as well…when the years of being his wife bring a closeness to him that surpasses any mother/son relationship. But until then….value her knowledge and understanding of her son and take advantage of it!

The Hand-Off

Your Family Doesn't Trump His

As we wrap up this chapter, we can't leave until we talk about family. Ahhh, the family. Everyone has one. That's the problem. Just kidding. Sorta. But seriously, family scenarios can really wreak havoc on a marriage, as well as put a strain on the mother-in-law/daughter-in-law relationship. But with a little sensitivity and intentionality, this doesn't have to be a source of contention in your relationship with your mother-in-law or your man.

The biggest truth to always keep in the forefront of your mind and heart is this…your

Your family can never or should never trump his family. And vice versa

The Hand-Off

family can never or should never trump his family. And vice versa. There are going to be a bazillion Thanksgivings, Christmas', births of babies, school events, and other fun happenings of life that both families will want to share in. Both families want and deserve time with you as a couple. It's very important to treat both families with the same respect when it comes to spending time with them.

Often, for some reason, time spent with the family of the wife trumps time spent with the family of the husband. I have heard from many mothers-in-law that they often feel left out or that they always get second best when it comes to holidays. Or they get told when festivities need to happen to accommodate the wife's family's plans. Or they aren't invited to come when a new baby arrives. They feel on the outside of the happenings of you and your husband's life while watching your family get a front row seat.

The Hand-Off

Whether it's the holidays, birthdays, births of babies, or another happy occasion, both sides of the family are longing to take part in you and your husband's life. Putting one family's plans ahead of the other family or giving access to one family more than the other is insensitive, inconsiderate, and goes against making the hand-off a success. If you are just starting out, this is the time to have a conversation about what is fair and how you and your husband will handle holidays and other events with each other's respective families.

You may be thinking, "Oh, but you have no idea how crazy his family is! I can't stand being around them!" Again, let me be frank…no matter how crazy they are, they are his family. They matter to him, therefore they better matter to you. You cannot go into a marriage planning on always giving preference to your family and leaving his family out. It

The Hand-Off

will produce much strife and put your man in the middle of an impossible battle. I'm not referring to situations where boundaries need to be set for an abusive and controlling family. I'm talking about when you just prefer to be with your family rather than his. If you can be honest and see yourself in this paragraph, please consider having a change of heart when it comes to including his family in your lives, just like you plan on doing with your family.

When Taylor and Madeline got married, we talked and agreed that the big holidays, Thanksgiving and Christmas, would be split. For instance, if they are with our family on Thanksgiving, then I know they will be with Madeline's family on Christmas. Therefore, we find another time to celebrate Christmas with them. Then the next year we switch; Taylor and Madeline go to her family's house at Thanksgiving and they are with us on Christmas.

The Hand-Off

When our granddaughter was born, my family was made to feel very welcome at the hospital and we made ourselves available to help in any way they needed. Madeline's family came into town and we, of course, let them have time with the kids alone. On the day Madeline came home from the hospital, we all ate dinner over at our house. In other words, we worked together and respected one another and here is the big thing....we communicated. Sometimes communication is all that is needed to avoid issues. Just talk.

If you share a town with both sets of families, I suggest a sit-down to just talk about how the holidays

Sometimes communication is all that is needed to avoid issues

and family events might work. Marriage is a joining of two families. Respect and honor are crucial on both sides. One family can't feel as though they have to fight for time with you and your husband, or always feel they are getting the leftovers.

Again, living with a mind-set that you now belong to his family, and he belongs to your family, helps in being fair as you share your life with both families. It's not, "I want to be with my family"… it's "Your family is my family and I want to be with them as well as mine." Your attitude will go a long way in helping your mother-in-law want to cooperate and work with your family's plans. It's just common courtesy and it doesn't have to be difficult.

The Hand-Off

So congratulations on going to the chapel! I am so excited for you! You are gaining a wealth of knowledge and resource in the gift of your mother-in-law. Remember to lead with graciousness as you move into that number one position in your man's life. Your mother-in-law will bless you as you consider, recognize, and acknowledge her role in helping him be the man you fell in love with. You can look forward to sharing the wonderful moments of life with your new family and inviting your husband into your family's traditions. So as the hand-off happens, reach out and receive the baton with grace, and understand the tear you might see on her cheek. She will love you for it.

Chapter 4: Reflection

Daughters-in-law, have you embraced the presence of your mother-in-law in your life? If so, what does this look like? If not, what steps are you willing to take to begin embracing her presence in your life with your husband and family?

Why do you think you tend to keep your mother-in-law at arms length? If it's something she has done, are you willing to have a gentle conversation with her and share your heart? Write down how you might begin that conversation. If it's because of hurts you have from your relationship with your own mother, are you willing to give your mother-in-law a chance to love you differently? What is one step you could take to begin to let her in and give her that chance?

Chapter Five

Healing the Great Divide

Not too long ago I was speaking about the hand-off at a conference. The room became very quiet at a certain point when I began to talk about the pain that is so prevalent in this relationship. It was as if every woman in the room could relate to what I was saying. We had laughed and had a little fun, but the laughter turned to tears for some in the room as we spoke about the frustration in misunderstanding, the strain in communication, and the pain that accompanies the heart when this relationship is broken.

The Hand-Off

At the beginning of this book I said I was FOR the both of you. I still am. I don't sit on the side of one more than the other. I am both a mother-in-law and a daughter-in-law. I understand the work, vulnerability, and intention involved in this relationship. I have heard stories from both sides and both are hurting. I don't hear more from the mother-in-law than the daughter-in-law. The struggle and pain seem to be evenly spread out between both. One is not to blame more than the other. It truly is often a struggle to be a mother-in-law and just as much a struggle to be a daughter-in-law.

If you are sitting in your relationship with your mother-in-law or daughter-in-law and you are hurting, I am thinking of you as I write this chapter. If you have been mistreated and have very little desire for relationship, please keep reading. If you can't see a path forward in your relationship...hopefully in the pages ahead, one will begin to light up.

The Hand-Off

All I ask is for you to please open your heart and invite a willingness to change to be your companion as you continue to read. Because the truth is, you have zero power to change her....but you have all the power in the world to change you.

> You have zero power to change her....but you have all the power in the world to change you

And even one simple change in you, can make a massive impact on her. It's humbling to change. But humble people are my most favorite people to be around.

There is no relationship that is healthy and good where there has not been a lot of work put into it. Every relationship requires something from us. If we want a good marriage, we have to work hard at serving, giving tons of grace, and loving well. I have a best friend, Tracie, and my relationship with her is healthy and good because we work hard at respecting one another, allowing each other to be who we are and we both put time and effort into the friendship.

More and more I am running into people whose relational life is a hot mess. It's not one of life and health, but rather dysfunction and pain. What I notice missing in a lot of people is the tenacity to stay in a relationship and work

Why aren't we willing to fight for friendship, to stay in and persevere through the hard for health and wholeness in our relationships?

through the issues that come up. I see the attitude of "I don't need this in my life." What they mean by "this" is "the inconvenience". The

The Hand-Off

inconvenience is clothed in having to be patient, giving up something you want, becoming good at listening, or actually caring about someone else's feelings more than your own. Whether it's a romantic relationship, a friendship, a neighbor relationship, or a family member…it seems to be easier to walk away and forfeit all the time, energy and love that has been put into the relationship than to stick with it, take a hard look within, be willing to listen, do some changing and come out with a stronger relationship.

Why are we choosing to walk away from so many relationships? Why aren't we willing to fight for friendship, to stay in and persevere through the hard for health and wholeness in our relationships? Why are we settling for so much less than is possible? Good relationships take work and effort…have we become that lazy?

The Hand-Off

Are you settling for less in this very important relationship with your mother-in-law or daughter-in-law? Have you had the attitude of "Whatever…" or "I can't do this anymore." or "She will never change." or "It's not worth it." You may have every right to feel the way you do. In fact, I am sure many of you have a very good reason to give up on this relationship ever being something of health and life.

I can say with confidence, if one of you is unhappy in the relationship, more than likely both of you are. It is not often that one describes the relationship as wonderful and the other describes it as horrible. Usually the one thing both can agree on is that the relationship is less than perfect. This is a great starting place.

The Hand-Off

In the admission and agreement that both of you are hurting and unhappy, there lies a hope that it can get better. The fact that you are both willing to admit things could be better should speak to both of you that no one is pointing all the fingers of blame to one person. It says you both understand that it takes two people to make a relationship all it can be. Because of this, there is great hope in healing the divide between you. So where can you start?

Perfecting the Art of Listening

How about listening? The art of being a good listener is a very underrated gift. Not everyone has mastered this valuable relational attribute. It's such a necessary ability to have in order to make any relationship healthy.

The Hand-Off

There is not one person
out there in a thriving,
whole and functional
relationship that doesn't
have listening skills high
on their list of priorities.

> **The art of being a good listener is a very underrated gift**

It's a must. This is where
the healing will begin…in the act of listening with the purpose of
understanding your mother-in-law or daughter-in-law's pain. Let me say
that again…the healing will begin when you choose to listen with the
purpose of understanding the other's pain.

When we can hear and understand someone's pain, when we can
empathize with it, when we can put our feelings aside and listen with
purpose, we will begin to see through a different set of glasses. If we

The Hand-Off

don't begin by listening with purpose to try to understand the other's pain, if we only agree to listen with the intent of reacting to their pain, and saying "our piece", we will not move forward, instead the movement will either be stalled, or move backwards.

If you are wanting to heal in this relationship, but are unwilling to listen with the purpose of understanding the other, it will be a waste of your time and hers to try to talk. It's not all about your pain. I don't doubt for one minute that you may be really, truly wounded, but she might be too. Coming into conversation with our guard up, ready to defend our actions and words with a list a mile long of our complaints and a memory of hurt that goes back years and years, will end the conversation before it even begins.

The Hand-Off

So how are your listening skills? Rather, let me ask this…what would your mother-in-law or daughter-in-law say about your listening skills? Remember that question I dared you to ask in chapter two…"What is it like to live on the other side of me?"

> ## What would your mother-in-law or daughter-in-law say about your listening skills?

This would be a good time to consider what it might be like to sit across from you and have a hard conversation.

A good listener has a few key rules they live by in conversations.

- They always maintain eye contact with who is talking
- They are aware of the facial expressions they are making as the person is speaking

The Hand-Off

- They resist the urge to roll their eyes or shake their heads as if to say "You have no idea what you are talking about!"
- As they listen, they nod as if to say "I hear what you are saying. I'm getting it."
- They force themselves to focus on what is being spoken instead of thinking about their response.
- Often times they will say this, "So what I hear you saying is _____, is this correct?"
- They NEVER interrupt.

So how do you fare? Do you recognize yourself in these descriptions? If there is a great divide right now in your relationship, there needs to be a conversation. Maybe even a few of them. If both of you agree to enter into a conversation, determined to be a good listener, then your chances are good for the relationship to move forward.

The Hand-Off

There could be many reasons why there is a great divide in your relationship with your mother-in-law or daughter-in-law. Perhaps it is simply a misunderstanding that needs to be talked through. Or maybe it's more serious and the struggle has roots to it that may take some time for healing to take place. However deep the problem goes, the first thing that must be dealt with and reestablished is trust.

Trust is a Must

There is a deep level of trust needed in this relationship. After all, this is not a casual relationship in your life. If you are a mother-in-law, your daughter-in-law holds a very important place in the heart of your son. If you are a daughter-in-law, your mother-in-law holds a very special place in the heart of your husband. This means you both need to have a special place in your heart for one another. This is a long-term relationship, one that must have a strong foundation of trust. Trust is the basis for all relationships. If you distrust, it means you don't have faith in her, you don't believe her and you don't take her at her word. This does not set up a landscape for a thriving and life giving relationship.

Remember…you are family. Family has each other's back. Trust can easily be broken if she knows you are talking about or complaining about her. Trust can be broken if you promise something and don't follow through. Trust can be damaged if you embarrass her in front of others. Trust can be affected if you are difficult to converse with, always disagreeing or spouting your opinion in an unattractive way. You have to earn her trust and the effort you expend earning it will determine the depth of that trust in this precious relationship. I have worked hard to earn Madeline's trust. It would break my heart if I did anything to damage what I have worked so hard to establish.

The Hand-Off

Have you lost trust in, or lost the trust of your mother-in-law or daughter-in-law? If so, the healing can only begin by addressing this issue before addressing anything else. Get the foundational issue dealt with first and you will find a lot of the other, less important things, will be solved too.

If you know broken trust is an issue, how do you begin talking it through? Why don't you begin by giving each other a chance to share what caused the fracture in the trust. Don't be surprised if something you feel is very insignificant is the very thing that upset her. Remember, you are both coming from very different perspectives. Respect this. You demonstrate this respect in your response to her sharing. Remember all those habits of a good listener? This is a good time to put them into use.

The Hand-Off

Your response to the woman sitting across from you is crucial as you listen well to her. Trust is not re-established by making empty promises or by trying to explain why she shouldn't feel that way, or make an excuse for what you said or did. You restore her trust by assuring her you have heard clearly what she has shared and

> **You restore her trust by assuring her you have heard clearly what she has shared and understand how that could have hurt her.**

understand how that could have hurt her. If an apology is needed, give a sincere apology. Do you know what I have learned about apologizing? It doesn't make a lick of difference if I meant to hurt someone or not…if I hurt someone intentionally or unintentionally, I need to say I am sorry. Period. A sincere, humble apology and giving them opportunity to forgive you can do more healing in a person's heart than anything else said. "I am so sorry, will you please forgive me?" Amazing, powerful words… when said from a sincere heart.

Being Willing to Forgive

When we find ourselves in a relationship where there is a great divide needing to be healed, not only do we find ourselves asking for forgiveness, but often times we are required to offer it as well. Asking for or offering…both can be hard. Both are humbling acts of kindness. Both are powerful and necessary in the healing process.

Remember…anything worth doing is worth the hard things required of us. The best of relationships have weathered difficult times. Apologies have been given and forgiveness offered in any healthy relationship. On several occasions, I have apologized to Madeline and asked her forgiveness for things I have felt I needed to address. Each time she has given what I haven't deserved…grace. I have done the same with my mother-in-law, Saundra. I can remember one time when I was sitting at the lunch table with my in-laws, and my mother-in-law said something and I corrected her in front of everyone at the table. I knew the moment the words were out of my mouth that I shouldn't have said them, but it was too late…they were out there. Later that afternoon I contacted her and told her I was sorry for correcting her in front of everyone and asked her to forgive me for

> **The best of relationships have weathered difficult times. Apologies have been given and forgiveness offered in any healthy relationship.**

embarrassing her in any way. She, being the gracious woman she is, forgave me immediately and all was well.

It is a gift to your soul to be willing to forgive. When we live with unforgiveness in our heart towards someone, it is like us drinking poison yet hoping the other person dies. Unforgiveness keeps us from love, strips us of peace, causing us to remain stuck in our pain. When we choose to offer grace and forgive an offense, it sets us free to love, to embrace peace, and release our pain.

> **When we live with unforgiveness in our heart towards someone, it is like us drinking poison yet hoping the other person dies.**

No one deserves to be forgiven. That's why it requires grace to forgive. Grace is being given what we don't deserve. To offer forgiveness is to offer grace. All of us will need grace in our lifetime. No one is perfect.

The Hand-Off

We all make mistakes, say things we shouldn't, and act in ways that are hurtful. When we choose to forgive, we are acknowledging that we too need grace. We offer grace because we are certain we will need it extended to us at some point.

It is far easier to offer forgiveness when we are asked, but sometimes we never get to hear the words "I'm sorry, will you forgive me?" It's in times like this when it's even harder to offer forgiveness. But in choosing to forgive, we don't do it for the other person, we do it for our own health and healing of soul.

If you have been hurt by your mother-in-law or daughter-in-law and need to forgive her, please don't wait for her to ask you. Right now, make a choice to offer her grace…to forgive her for the hurtful actions or words.

The Hand-Off

Keep in mind that the hurtful actions or words may have come from a place of fear, pain, uncertainty, or from a fragile place you are unaware of in her. This will allow you to live your life free from resentment and bitterness towards her. It will help you love her in the way that will draw her to you. Some day she might come and ask for your forgiveness, and won't it be wonderful to say "I've already forgiven you, but thank you so much for asking."

Making a Way Forward

Once you have acknowledged both parties play a part in the great divide and have willingly sat down and listened with open hearts, asked for and given forgiveness which has allowed trust to begin to be restored, it is time to forge a new path in your relationship. Moving forward in relationship means changing some thought patterns, implementing new habits of communication and showing appreciation for one another in new and creative ways. It will take the effort of both of you to turn your relationship into something new…something treasured…something precious to you both. Let's talk about what these things look like in a practical way.

Changing thought patterns about her can be challenging. If you have lived with a strained relationship, your thoughts have probably leaned more on the negative side. It is now time to intentionally begin to think of her with new thoughts. Here are some suggestions on how to begin doing just that.

- Write down all of the good character traits you see in her. You may have to look deep. You may have to be generous. That is okay. Look deep, be generous. Refer back to this list when you are needing to be reminded of her strengths.

The Hand-Off

- When you know you are going to see her or talk to her, expect it to go well. Beforehand think about how you want your tone of voice and facial expressions to be. Remember, you want her to feel invited by you into your life. Be inviting.
- When she says or does something to irritate you or hurt you, try to remember the progress you have made. If needed, address it with her right then. Use very kind and soft words, assuring her you value the relationship and want it to be good.
- Think the best of her. Give her the benefit of the doubt. Don't assume she meant to hurt you. She is learning to change also. Give continual grace when needed as you think thoughts about her. Push negative thoughts aside and let positive and truthful thoughts be what you dwell on.

Implementing new habits of communicating is an important step in moving forward in relationship. It can also be a challenge to change these habits, but keep in front of you the

Keep in front of you the picture of the kind of relationship you want with her

picture of the kind of relationship you want with her. She is worth changing for. You are worth changing for. The relationship will thrive under the work of creating new habits of communication with each other. Here are some suggestions.

- Always talk to her the way you would want to be spoken to. Do you like to be spoken to with respect? Do you like for someone to smile and laugh with you?

The Hand-Off

- Greet her with enthusiasm. Whether you are calling her, texting her, or greeting her in person, help her feel like you are so happy to be talking to her!

- Engage her in friendly banter. The relationships that are most fun are those where laughter is often present. Don't be afraid to act silly, show her something you found humorous, tell her a funny story. This may be a bit of a stretch if your relationship has always been of a serious nature. It will take intention to lighten it up!

- Use loving words. Mothers-in-law…affectionate names like sweetheart, hon, sweet girl, when spoken or written go deep and make your daughter-in-law feel loved by you. Daughters-in-law…loving inquiries like "How have you been?" "How have you been feeling?" "What's been new with you?" speak to your mother-in law's heart that you sincerely care about her as a person.

The Hand-Off

Showing your appreciation and love in new and creative ways will help take your relationship to a whole new level. Being willing to put effort into showing how you care makes your caring words believable. Anyone can say kind words, but backing them up with action takes the meaning of them to new heights and helps build that bridge of trust in the relationship again. Here are some suggestions to how you can creatively show your love and appreciation to one another.

- Send a short text or write a small note simply saying "Hey! Just thinking of you and hope you are having a great day!" It could change the course of her entire day.
- When you see a small gift that reminds you of her, buy it and give it to her. The reality that you know her tastes, and thought of her will touch her heart deeply. This could be as simple as buying her favorite candy bar!
- Send her or bring her a plant. It will be a reminder to her every time she waters it that you thought of her. It will make her smile.

- Brag about her in front of others while she is around to hear it. "My mother-in-law makes the most delicious chocolate cake you have ever eaten!" "My daughter-in-law is an amazing mom!

I want to close this chapter with encouragement to those who are in a relationship that has a great divide, yet the other person

We live in the decisions WE make

has no interest in healing it. There is a lot of hope for you. We live with the decisions WE make. You can begin to be a better listener and make intentional strides to build trust with her. You can choose to forgive her and live out that grace towards her. You can begin to put into action some of the suggestions made to change your thought patterns towards her, improve communication with her, and show her more effectively your love for her. Remember...you have a lot of power in your hands.

The Hand-Off

She does not determine how you treat her. You do. You and you alone decide what kind of a person you want to be. She will notice and no matter what anyone says, the change in you will impact her, whether you begin to see her soften or not. But you can move forward feeling at peace about the role you play in the relationship.

I hope this chapter has helped point you in the right direction in healing and given you both hope that things can be better. It may not always be an easy journey, but at the end of the road, you will have a relationship that is healthier, happier, and one you both can cherish.

Chapter 5: Reflection

I'm including several questions and challenges for this chapter. Remember...you only have the power to change you, not her. Moving forward is the goal and even without her cooperation, moving forward is possible.

What role have you played in the pain that is currently in your relationship? Are you willing to take responsibility for your actions? Apologize if needed?

What steps can you take to become a better listener?

The Hand-Off

Have you caused your mother-in-law/daughter-in-law to lose trust in you? If so, what steps can you take to begin to earn that trust back? Do you need to apologize? Ask for forgiveness?

In what area of your relationship can you begin to offer more grace? Are you willing to forgive her, even if she hasn't asked for your forgiveness? Remember…you forgive more for your sake than for hers. It will set you free.

The Hand-Off

Chapter Six

The Man in the Middle

We are going to switch things up in this chapter, as it is written to the man in the middle of this mother-in-law/daughter-in-law relationship. As you read these next few pages, I hope as you hear me encourage him in his role, you begin to understand the very precarious position he sits in, especially if there are issues surrounding your relationship with one another.

The Hand-Off

Dear Husband and Son,

You, my fine fellow, have found yourself in love with a woman you want to spend the rest of your life with and I dare say you haven't given your mother much thought! Don't worry, you are quite normal! Most men are not thinking about their mother when they are falling in love.

Whether you are just starting out with your new wife, or have been married for years and have been stuck in the middle of a seemingly helpless feud between your wife and mother, this chapter is

> ## You have in your hands an incredible amount of power in the love of these two women

written to you. Hopefully it will help you avoid some pitfalls if you are

The Hand-Off

newly married or help you navigate your role in this relationship between your mother and wife more effectively.

The truth is, you are loved. Your mother has loved you since the moment she set eyes on you, and your wife has loved you since you convinced her you were worthy of her. You have in your hands an incredible amount of power in the love of these two women, who both think you pretty much hung the moon! You may feel like you don't have a lot of influence when it comes to their relationship but trust me...you do. The way in which you talk about your mother, will influence the way your wife will come to think and feel about her. The same is true with the way in which you talk about your wife to your mother. So please be thoughtful in the way you represent each of them to one another. It can make all the difference in the world in how smooth the hand-off goes and life after the hand-off!

The Hand-Off

When your Mother Struggles to Let You Go

Let's begin with how you can go about interacting with your wife in regard to her relationship with your mother, especially if the hand-off was a rocky one. If you read Chapter Three, you learned about the challenge it can be for your mother to hand your heart off to your new wife. If you have never thought about what it was like for your mother when you to fell in love and got married, now is the time. It is important for you to understand she has held your heart and protected it fiercely since the day you were born. Handing it off and trusting your wife with it was not easy. Even a secure, emotionally healthy mother can find it hard to watch another woman move into the spot she has held for her son's entire life, but it's imperative she lets go completely of you and gives plenty of room for your wife to settle into her new role. Some women struggle more than others when their son marries. If your mother happens to be one of them, we will talk later about how you can be a great help in making the hand-off easier.

Hopefully your mother was able to completely let you go and place your heart fully into your wife's capable hands. If not, your wife could be feeling the weight of dragging your mother behind her as she refuses to let go of you. This could hinder warm, fuzzy feelings to well up towards your mother, and who could blame her? Your mother has been, if your relationship was a good one, the number one woman in your life, but it is now time for your wife to be number one. How does she move into that spot when your mother is struggling to step out of it? How can you help your wife move graciously into that number one spot?

The needs and wishes of your wife matter a lot. You live with her, you want her to be happy. If she's not happy, you're not happy. It's hard to be your wife and hold on to your heart when she can't get your mother to let go of it. But you can help your wife understand the gift your mother handed her when she handed her your heart. You can help your wife appreciate what your heart meant to your mother. You can help her understand how hard this might be for your mother and encourage your wife to be gracious. Her attitude towards the hand-off makes a difference and determines her heart and her treatment towards your mother. Has your wife been gracious? If not, you have the power to encourage her in becoming so.

How do you go about encouraging her in this way? She loves you, so hopefully you have chosen a woman who listens out of

> **Make sure your wife knows your love for your mother remains but does not trump your love for her**

her love for you. As you assure her with words of your dedication to her, helping her rest in the truth that your mother is not someone she is in competition with for your love, she will see how much your mother means to your heart, and want to respect this woman who has helped make you into the man she fell in love with. Make sure your wife knows your love for your mother remains but does not trump your love for her. Assure her with convincing words that she is the first priority in your heart and life, and nothing will change that.

These words will not mean anything if you don't back them up with action. Some mothers think they should have access to their son anytime they want or need him, even after he is married. This is a sign she hasn't completely let go. But the truth is, your wife takes precedent over your mother's desire to see or talk to you, or her demands on your time. At times you have to say, "Mom, we aren't able to come this weekend. We have plans." Or, "I'm sorry, Mom. I am not available today but later this week I can come by." A healthy wife understands your mother matters a lot and needs your attention at times, especially if your dad is not in the picture and she lives alone. But when your wife sees she is first and you're not running off every time your mother calls, she will be able to keep her heart and attitude towards your mother in a good place.

Now what about your mother? What if she is still clinging to your heart, trying valiantly to maintain her number one status in your life and struggling to step down to her number two place? What can you do to help her? We have mentioned setting boundaries with her regarding your time and attention, but how else can you help reassure her that letting go of you is a good thing?

The Hand-Off

In most cases, all that is needed is an honest conversation full of assurances of your love as well as confidently laying out your intentions of loving your wife with your whole heart, reminding your mother she is the one who taught you how to do that. If you haven't learned this already about women, we do better when we are dealt with honestly, practically, and directly. Help your mother see that the addition of your wife to the family is a wonderful bonus of more love, more adventure, and more joy. Just like you assured your wife of your love for her, assure your mother that although she is no longer in the number one spot, your love for her has not diminished. Thank her for all the love she poured into you and for teaching you what love looks like, so that you can be the husband your wife deserves. If this loving conversation doesn't have the effect you were hoping it would on your mother's attitude towards your new wife and marriage, it will have to be backed up with some very clearly spelled out boundaries.

The Hand-Off

As an example of what I am referring to, I know a young couple where the mother thought she could treat her son's new wife with unkindness, harsh words, and demands that were unreasonable. Her son took her aside, informing her that his wife was his first priority now and treating her like that was not ever acceptable. If she wanted to have a relationship with them, she would have to change the way she treated his wife. After a few times of pulling his mother aside and laying clear boundaries, she got the message and began to treat the wife better.

When Your Wife wants Nothing to do with Your Family

One complaint I have heard from several mothers-in-law is that it seems their son has little to no say-so about how she is treated by the daughter-in-law. The daughter-in-law's feelings about the mother-in-law and/or his family stand alone and is the deciding factor in how much contact and time is given to the son's side of the family. The son is obviously in the middle, wanting peace in his home, and feels like he needs to support his wife. This is true, but shouldn't there be a time when he should be heard, if he feels his mother/family is being left out or ill-treated? It's in situations like this when it's time to set boundaries with your wife, instead of your mother. It's imperative that you are clear about how important continuing a

Let it be made clear that you have no intention of putting off relationships with your mother or other family members

relationship with your mother and family is to you. It's important your wife knows she is loved and adored by you, but that you also are concerned about your family's feelings. If your mother/family has done something hurtful or spiteful to your wife, then naturally you would be called to set very clear boundaries of how you expect your wife to be treated. If your wife, though, is of the attitude that she just doesn't want your mother/family around and a part of your life for no apparent reason, or she just prefers her family, this too must be addressed. Let it be made clear that you have no intention of putting off relationships with your mother or other family members.

If it comes to it and your wife simply will not comply with being decent and kind, then you can have relationship with your mother and family outside of her. Some may disagree, but I don't think a wife has a right to cut off her husband's mother or other family if they have done nothing to deserve such treatment. Submitting to this unkindness and allowing her to destroy your relationship with your family, is just as much your fault as it is hers for acting in such an indecent way.

The Hand-Off

I have a friend who lives with this exact situation. Her son married a woman who has wanted nothing to do with her ever since the wedding. My friend and her husband have tried to sit down and get to the bottom of the problem. They have apologized for anything they might have done to hurt her and they have bent over backwards to make it easy for a relationship. They have received

> **Both your wife and your mother need you to help them love each other well.**

nothing…absolutely nothing. They hardly have a relationship with their four grandchildren because they feel like imposters anytime they visit. The biggest dagger to my friend's heart is how her son has succumbed to his wife's wishes and has so easily seemed to cast her and her husband aside. They were a very close family and had a wonderful relationship with their son before he was married. But because he has not fought for a relationship with them, it breaks her heart in the most devastating way as any mother can imagine.

I understand this young husband and father is caught in the middle, but there is a point when it's okay to say to your wife, "I want a relationship with my family. I want my children to know my parents. They are my children too. If you don't want to have any relationship with them, I cannot and won't force you to, but I will have a relationship with them and so will our children." It's sad to me there are situations out there like this, but the more I talk about the relationship between mothers-in-law and daughters-in-law, the more situations I hear that are similar to the one I described. I realize sometimes you have very little recourse if your home life is to be one of any kind of peace, but it is disheartening to me to hear mother's stories of such disconnect from their son's life because of the woman he chose to marry.

The Hand-Off

As we finish up this chapter, I hope you have discovered how important your role is as you sit in the middle of this relationship between your mother and your wife. They both need you to help them love each other well. They need you reminding them at times what a gift the other is to their life. Building them both up in the others' eyes will do wonders for this relationship. Refusing to talk badly about either one with the other will show your love and respect for them both. Use your influence wisely, and your life will be a peaceful one as your mother and wife live in a beautiful relationship with one another.

Chapter 6: Reflection

Can you identify any way in which you have contributed to putting your son or husband in the middle of your relationship with your daughter-in-law or mother-in-law?

What steps can you take to make it easier on your son? Husband? When it comes to living in the middle of your relationship with one another?

Epilogue

I want to close this book with Kathy and Heather's story. I hope it touches your heart in a way that helps you lay down any hurts or personal rights you feel you have in this relationship between you and your mother-in-law or daughter-in-law. I heard this story while in the middle of writing this book and knew I had to include it. It had such an impact on me and spoke of the power of the mother-in-law/daughter-in-law relationship like no other story I had heard. I have heard a lot of stories with pain and sadness, and anger attached to them, but this story only has love attached to it. Let it speak to your heart in a deep way and say whatever it is you may need to hear.

The Hand-Off

This is Kathy and Heather's story

Heather came into Kathy's life when Kathy's son Josh was in junior high school. Josh and Heather had become friends and soon Heather's journey and story was unveiled. Heather's mother had left soon after she was born. Her life was shadowed with ongoing abuse and dysfunction. Josh and Heather developed an unbreakable bond. He was someone she could hold tight to, trust and she found stability in his friendship and care. When they graduated high school, Josh and Heather eloped, an act that surprised no one.

For the next ten years, they both worked hard in careers and at night Heather went to school to earn her Masters Degree in Counseling. Recognizing the long-term and sometime never ending affects of growing up under the cloud of abuse and dysfunction, Heather's heart was to help girls like herself navigate the feelings of confusion, rage, and guilt that comes with recovery. She strived to make a difference, even to just one girl who was betrayed and abandoned by the people who should have protected her.

During this time, Josh and Heather decided to start their own family, something Heather so desperately wanted; the chance to provide unconditional love to a child of her own. Shortly into their first pregnancy, as she excitedly waited to hear the first heartbeat, the words came, "I'm sorry, the baby is dead." Heather continued staring at the monitor hoping that the heartbeat might suddenly appear, that there was a mistake, but there was only silence.

Heather suffered six more miscarriages as she and Josh tried to start their family. The loss of a baby, even early on, is a shock like no other. The

The Hand-Off

impact is like that of a wrecking ball. Each time Heather layed on the examining table watching the the screen, listening for the heartbeat, waiting for different words…then, I'm sorry.

For Josh and Heather, it never got easier; because how could it? And then for Heather, she had to continually struggle with the internal accusations of incompetency. Her body has failed at it's most natural function: motherhood.

With no mother, who was Heather to turn to? Who could she explain her grief, her paralyzing pain and her unending tears to?

Soon after Josh and Heather's 10th wedding anniversary, Heather was diagnosed with Stage 1 Ovarian cancer. Again, her body fails her.

The Hand-Off

Determined to fight with all that she had, Heather took an experimental radiation treatment that put the cancer into remission.

With a pile of medical bills, Josh and Heather moved into his mother, Kathy, and her hsuband's house hoping to pay off the medical bills. After a year, Josh unceremoniously decided he no longer wanted to be married and left, leaving nothing but pain, disbelief and anger behind.

Two month later, as Heather struggled to determine what to do with her life and where to go next, she found out the cancer had returned and it was already at Stage 4. With gracious hearts, Kathy and her husband asked Heather to continue to stay with them. This way, Kathy could help take care of her, go to appointments and, most importantly, be her security during this time.

The Hand-Off

Heather and Kathy grew close, very close. Through the many bedside conversations, whether at Kathy's home or the many hospital stays, they discovered a different side to each other and their relationship grew deep. It wasn't unusual for Kathy to crawl up into bed with Heather to comfort her and hold her as only a mother can do. Like the mother Heather never had. When Heather passed away, she left a huge part of herself with her mother-in-law, Kathy. And, Heather left this world finally knowing the love that she had so desperately craved.

At Heather's funeral, Kathy shared how she had the privilege of being called "Mom" by all eight of her children, as well as by Heather. She described Heather as "my person" and I was "her person." Kathy said she took no greater joy than caring for her in her last year of life and having the honor of being Heather's earthly "Mom." Unconditional love.

The Hand-Off

If I had the power, I would touch each of your hearts with the kind of love Kathy and Heather shared. I would open your heart and fill it with a longing to be who your mother-in-law or daughter-in-law needs you to be. When the curtain falls for any one of us, we aren't going to care about anything but people. All our frustrations and complaints of each other that drove us up a wall are all of a sudden going to become like dust, blown away with a simple breath and what will matter, what will last… is love.

CPSIA information can be obtained
at www.ICGtesting.com
Printed in the USA
BVHW060534091220
594995BV00004B/12

9 780578 688343